Exploring Earth's Resources

Using Rocks

Sharon Katz Cooper

Heinemann Library
Chicago, Illinois

Designed by Michelle Lisseter
Printed and bound in China, by South China Printing Company

11 10 09 08 07
10 9 8 7 6 5 4 3 2 1

Library of Congress Cataloging-in-Publication Data

Katz Cooper, Sharon.
  Using rocks / Sharon Katz Cooper.
      p. cm. -- (Exploring Earth's resources)
  Includes index.
  ISBN-13: 978-1-4034-9312-5 (lib. bdg.)
  ISBN-10: 1-4034-9312-X (lib. bdg.)
  ISBN-13: 978-1-4034-9320-0 (pbk.)
  ISBN-10: 1-4034-9320-0 (pbk.)
  1. Rocks--Juvenile literature. I. Title.
  QE432.2.K38 2007
  552--dc22

                                        2006029662

Acknowledgments
The publishers would like to thank the following for permission to reproduce photographs:
Alamy pp. **6** (blickwinkel), **18** (Dennis Macdonald), **19** (ImageState), **21** (image 100), **10**
(Interfoto Pressebildagentur); Corbis pp. **4** (Robert Harding World Imagery), **16**, **17** (Ecoscene);
Geoscience Features Picture Library pp. **14** top and bottom, **15**; Getty Images pp. **9** (Photodisc
Red), **12**, (photodisc), **13** (Jack Dykinga); Photolibrary **20** (Brandx Pictures); Science Photo
Library pp. **5** (Mauro Fermariello), **9** (Sinclair Stammers), **11** (Doug Martin); Still Pictures pp.
7, **9.**

Cover photograph reproduced with permission of Getty Images (Medio Images).

Every effort has been made to contact copyright holders of any material reproduced in
this book. Any omissions will be rectified in subsequent printings if notice is given to the
publishers.

Contents

Some words are shown in bold, **like this**.
You can find them in the glossary on page 23.

What Are Rocks?

Earth is made of rocks.

Rocks are underneath soil and grass. They are underneath water.

Rocks are a **natural resource**.

Natural resources come
from Earth.

What Are Rocks Made Of?

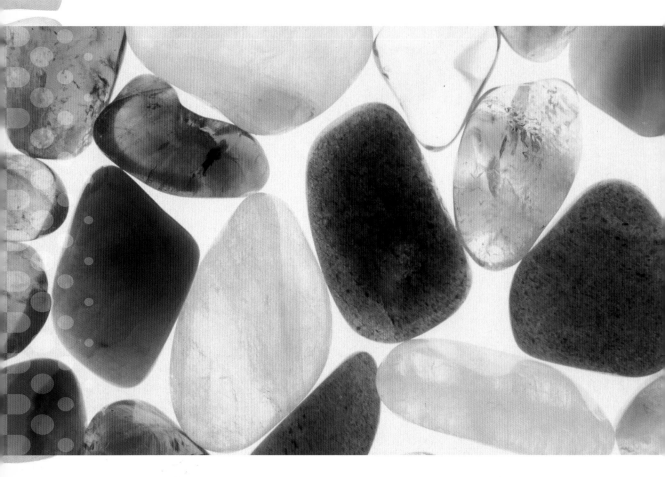

Rocks are made of different **minerals**.

Minerals are natural materials that are not alive.

iron

The minerals in a rock change how it looks and feels.

Iron is a mineral. Rocks with iron in them are hard.

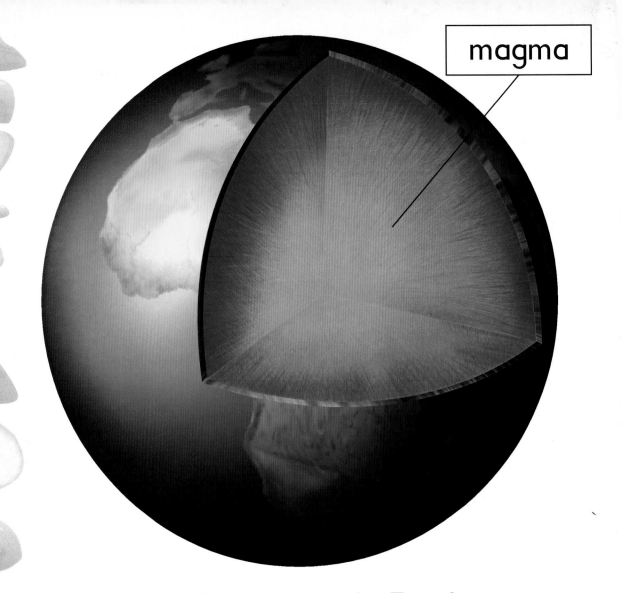

magma

Liquid rock deep inside Earth is called **magma**.

Magma cools and hardens slowly inside Earth.

granite

It forms rocks such as granite.

How Are Rocks Formed?

magma

Sometimes **magma** pours out of volcanoes. It becomes hard very quickly.

obsidian

It forms rocks such as obsidian.
Obsidian is very smooth, like glass.

Wind and water break big rocks into smaller pieces.

Stones and pebbles are small pieces of rock.

Soil and sand are tiny pieces of rock.

Layers of soil and sand pile up and become hard. They can form a new kind of rock.

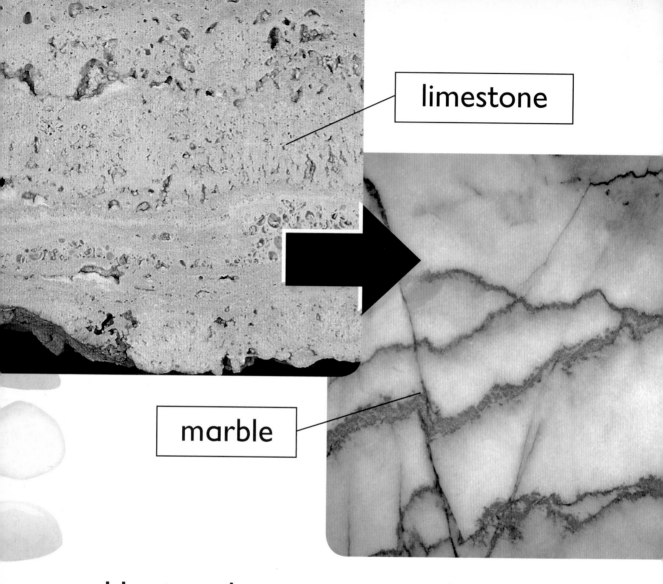

limestone

marble

Heat and **pressure** can change rock.

Very hot temperatures change limestone into marble.

14

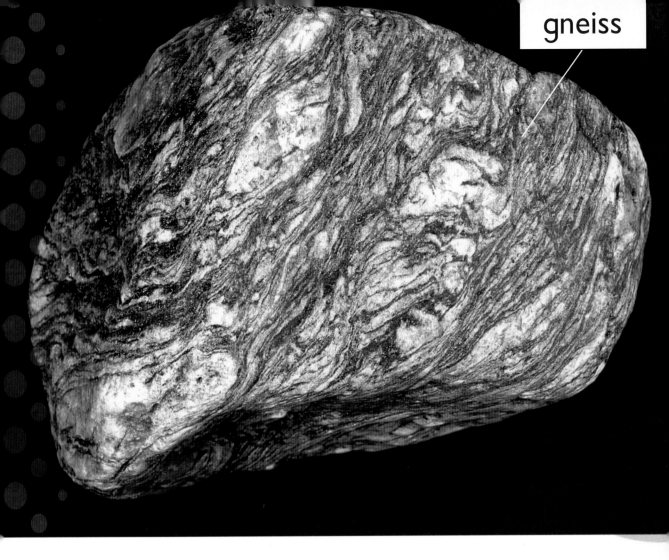

gneiss

Rocks like gneiss have very flat layers.

Pressure formed these layers in the rocks over time.

Where Do We Find Rocks?

Some rocks are easy to find.

They can be cut from the side
of mountains or cliffs.

Some rocks are only found deep
in Earth.

We have to dig down to get them out.

How Do We Use Rocks?

We use small pieces of rock to make roads.

A road has many layers of rock underneath.

We use big pieces of rock to build
things. Marble is a strong rock.

Buildings made of marble last
a long time.

We use very soft rocks to make plaster.

Plaster makes walls smooth.

Some rocks are very hard and beautiful. They are rare.

We use them to make jewelry.

Rock Collection

Scientists who study rocks are called geologists.

You can be a geologist in your own classroom or backyard. Look for different types of rock. Use the key to find out what they are.

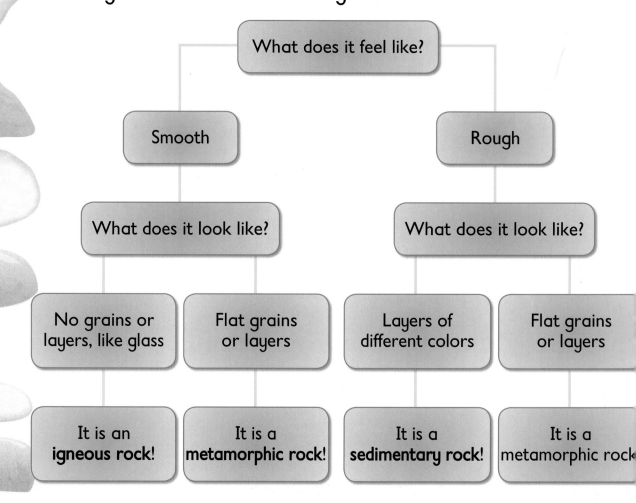

What does it feel like?

Smooth

Rough

What does it look like?

What does it look like?

No grains or layers, like glass

Flat grains or layers

Layers of different colors

Flat grains or layers

It is an **igneous rock!**

It is a **metamorphic rock!**

It is a **sedimentary rock!**

It is a metamorphic rock

Glossary

 **igneous rock** type of rock made when a volcano explodes

 **magma** liquid rock under Earth's surface

 **metamorphic rock** type of rock made when other rock gets very hot under the ground

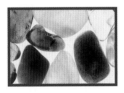 **mineral** non-living material from Earth

 **natural resource** material from Earth that we can use

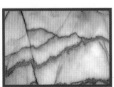 **pressure** pushing or squeezing on something

 **sedimentary rock** type of rock made when mud, sand, or sea creatures fall to the bottom of the sea

Index